The Minimalist Lifestyle Ultimate Guide!

Minimalist

Simplifying And Decluttering Your Life To Increase Happiness And Contentment, Focus, Time Management, And Improve Relationships!

I0428323

Ryan Cooper

STOP!!! Before you read any further....Would you like to know the secrets of Anti-Aging?

If your answer is yes, then you are not alone. Thousands of people are looking for the secret to reducing wrinkles, looking younger, and maintaining a youthful appearance.

If you have been searching for these answers without much luck, you are in the right place!

Not only will you gain incredible insight in this book, but because I want to make sure to give you as much value as possible, right now for a limited time you can get full **100% FREE access to a VIP bonus EBook** entitled **Anti-Aging Made Easy!**

Just Go Here For Free Instant Access:

www.LuxyLifeNaturals.com

Legal Notice

Disclaimer Notice

Table Of Contents

Introduction

I want to thank you and congratulate you for purchasing the book, *"Minimalist: The Minimalist Lifestyle Ultimate Guide! Simplifying And Decluttering Your Life To Increase Happiness And Contentment, Focus, Time Management, And Improve Relationships!"*

This book contains proven steps and strategies on how to improve your life through the ways of the minimalist.

Many of us put value in the things that we own, and while this is only understandable, too much value put on things can be a dangerous thing to hold. Most of us spend our lives giving up things and letting go of opportunities just so we could work and earn to buy things and possessions.

A nice house with a beautiful garden, a stylish car, the latest clothes and accessories, high-tech gadgets and electronics, or even gourmet dishes and trips around the world are just some of the things that people put value on. While all of these are good and well to have, the problem is when people give up what they should value more just to get these so-called luxuries and dreams. Those who have jobs and careers spend most of their time working and away from their families and loved ones, and the ones with their businesses tire themselves day and night so that they can achieve the success that they want.

Learn the ways of the minimalist and understand what are truly important in life. Written here are some strategies and tips on how you can declutter your space, your life, and how you can be more productive with the ways of the minimalist.

Thanks again for purchasing this book, I hope you enjoy it!

Chapter 1: What Does It Mean To Live A Minimalist Lifestyle?

What does it mean to live a minimalist lifestyle? If you are someone who is interested in a minimalist life or is simply intrigued by what minimalism is all about, you will find that the definition of living in a minimalist manner is anything but simple. Some people simply define minimalism as having less than a hundred things to own, while others say that it is all about living in the smallest house possible with the least number of things. Others will say that living a minimalist lifestyle is about removing the distractions and unnecessary things in life, while others will go so far as to say that it is all about getting rid of your things and not buying often enough to replace them.

These definitions and perhaps misconceptions are not surprising to hear because most people who say that they live minimalist lifestyles do indeed support such ideas. Most minimalists do not own a house or a car. If they do own a house, it will probably be one of the smallest and barest you have ever seen in your life. Most minimalist also do not own luxuries such as the latest gadgets like cell phones and laptops, while others do not even have a television in their place. There is also the general idea that minimalists do not have a job or if they do, they work the least number of hours possible. Others see minimalists as those how do nothing but write or read all day, probably working on their online businesses or their blogs. Whatever idea you may have of what a minimalist is or whatever you may have heard about these people, one thing for sure is that in one way or another, you will probably think of them as weirdos. Weird often has a negative connotation, but in this case, it can simply mean that, well, they are different.

Two minimalists who wrote a book about living a meaningful life with less define minimalism as a tool that can help you achieve freedom. There is freedom to be had from worries, from guilt, and even from the consumer culture that all of us live by if we try and apply minimalism to our lives. Summed up in one sentence, they define minimalism as 'a tool used to rid oneself of the excesses of life so that one may focus on what is important and therefore achieve happiness, freedom, and fulfillment.

Chapter 2: Overcoming Fear Of Letting Go Of Stuff And Other Things Cluttering Your Life

In another minimalist's words, minimalism is simply getting rid of the things that are not needed and those that are hardly ever used. This allows a person to live in a simple and uncluttered environment, and to live a simple and uncluttered life. At the core of this definition is the fact that minimalism is also about living without obsessions, and this means being able to overcome the fear of letting go of the things that clutter life.

Clutter can be defined as anything that no longer has any use, or anything that you no longer love, or anything that simply becomes a disorganized mess in your home. There is also the spiritual and emotional type of clutter, which are those that drain you of your energy and cause you pain as you think about them. While it is obviously harder to let go of sentiments that prove to be emotional clutters, physical clutters can be gotten rid of if you learn to let go of the fear of losing them. These fears stem from many reasons that can differ from one person to another, if you have these fears, know that you can do something about them.

- Fear of having to buy replacements – many people fear letting go of the things that clutter their lives, the things that even they know they no longer need, because they feel that they will have to find replacements. There is this pressure that when you let go of something, you have to get a replacement in return. This can cost money, and not everyone has the money to just buy new things. Let go of this fear by knowing that you do not have to buy replacements. If the clutter is something you have not used for a long time, then it is clear that you can live without it.

- Fear of wasting the money you used to buy them – people invest money on the things that they own and this is one of the main reasons why it is hard to let go of such things. Getting rid of the clutter feels almost similar to throwing away the money you have spent on it. Think again: you have used that thing enough for it to give back the money you spent. It is enough to enjoy the things you own, but once you no longer find use for them, learn to let go.

Keeping clutter can even cost you more money if they have to be maintained and taken care of. If you are worried about money, why not sell the items you need to get rid of? One man's trash is another's treasure.

- Fear of being left unprepared – there are those who feel safe with all the possessions that they have. After all, owning things makes you prepared for when you might need them. However, this can keep you from de-cluttering your life. Again, remember that clutter are those that you hardly use and almost never need. There are some items that you probably only use once a year or even less. If this is the case, then maybe you don't actually need them after all.

- Fear of letting go as being too much work – some people are set on removing the clutter from their houses and their lives, but they think that they do not have the time or energy to do so. Letting go of clutter means looking for somewhere to transfer your clutter, and this can be challenging. Put creativity into it and try to think of ways other than throwing them out. Have a garage sale or donate to charity. Go where you think your things will be more needed and it will only take a few minutes before your clutter is off of your hands. If you don' do this, you will spend more time and energy in keeping these things when they hardly have any use anymore.

Chapter 3: Do I Have To Be A Weirdo To Live Like A Minimalist And Enjoy The Minimalist Life?

Have you ever had the pleasure of earning your first paycheck? You then get excited and giddy over all the possibility that you can do with your hard-earned money. You now have money to go out with your friends on trips or to watch movies every weekend, or to treat yourself to a nice restaurant or even a relaxing massage. Most people would splurge on the latest gadgets and fashions, while some would jump at the chance of having their own vehicle even if it means spending a couple hundred dollars every week.

This is the normal course of action that majority of people take, but minimalists do not work in the same way. Instead, they probably earn less than the normal person, they hardly splurge on clothes or the latest gadgets, and they are happy with the simplest home-cooked meal they can come up with. These people are the ones who would rather stay at home than go out with friends, and in most cases, are the ones that others refer to as weird. But what makes them weird? Is it because they are simply different?

Living a minimalist lifestyle is truly different from the norm, but it does not have to be weird. The term 'weird' has a negative connotation and minimalism does not have to be negative. Sure people may call you weird if you do not have a cell phone or a computer or even a television set. They may think you a weirdo if you only own one pair of pants and five shirts at the most. But then again, can someone not live a normal and happy life with so little?

Minimalists may not enjoy the same type of luxury that other people do. They may not go to the movies, they may not dine at fancy restaurants, and they may hardly go shopping, but they can still be normal happy people.

Will you treat your friends differently if you own and spend less? Yes, you will miss out on the things that they spend on, but you can still enjoy chatting with them and sharing stories, or going on walks or even exchanging books and other things that you find interesting.

Being a minimalist does mean that you live differently, but it does not mean that you have to live by yourself and that you have a non-existent social life. Some may call you boring, others may think you are a party pooper, but there is more to people than just the things that they own or the things that they can pay for. In fact, minimalists claim that they are even happier with a minimalist lifestyle because they found what is truly valuable and important in life.

To quote world-renowned sociologist Elise Boulding, *'The Consumption society has made us feel that happiness lies in having things, and has failed to teach us the happiness of not having things.'*

Chapter 4: How Can Everyday People Incorporate And Benefit From Minimalist Living?

A normal life and even happiness can be achieved from minimalist living. Even if you are not sure if you would ever want to be a minimalist, there are certain values that can benefit you if you choose to live a minimalist lifestyle.

- Knowing What is Important

Minimalists have a better view of what is truly important in life. This is because they are able to get rid of the clutter all around them. The things that you hardly use, or those that you do use simply because they are around you, can block you from the things that truly matter. Through minimalist living, people have a better idea of what they can truly live without and what are the more important things in life. Especially in today's world where everyone is stressed over a hundred different reasons, living a minimalist lifestyle allows you to forego all those that are less than essential. Instead, focus more the things that truly matter.

- Time for What Matters

Aside from knowing what matters the most, a minimalist lifestyle also allows you to have time for the more important things in life. It is a cliché story where a parent knows that the most important thing in life is family, and yet he or she chooses to slave away at work, not having enough time to be with the kids or the loved one. In minimalist living, there is more with less as the less clutter you have, the more time you get in return. This time is well-spent being focused on the things that do matter instead of on those that simply clutter one's life.

- Being More Carefree

Stress comes from materialism. People stress themselves over how they can buy whatever they want and how they should take care of such things and what else they need to buy in order to maintain these things properly. Materialism has brought us to a state of life where enough is never enough, and the more you have, the more you seem to need. But these worries are focused simply on the material things and not on the person or the things that matter. If people learn to detach themselves from material things, they can worry less and have greater peace of mind.

- Being More Productive

Minimalist living focuses on developing the self and allowing one to thrive even without material possessions. This allows the person to take greater risks, to go after what is more important, and to improve oneself to the fullest. Productivity is not measured in terms of earnings or possessions. Instead, a minimalist is productive in the way that he or she is more fulfilled, and in being so, the minimalist has more to offer to the people and the world around them.

- Being Free

Material possessions lead to stress, worries, and even fear. We fear that we never have enough, we fear that the things we own can one day be taken from us, and so we slave away so that we can always earn to buy more of the things that bring temporary happiness and a lifetime of stress. Learning to let go of these things allows a minimalist to be free: free to do the things he or she truly wants and freedom to be who you really are without fear.

Chapter 5: Does Living Like A Minimalist Really Make You Happier And Give You More Contentment? – Becoming More Aware Of Your Surroundings

Two guys by the name of Joshua Fields Millburn and Ryan Nicodemus are quite known in the world of minimalism. They are both authors of their own blogs and a book entitled Minimalism: Live a Meaningful Life, earn an annual income of about $40,000, and are both at the ripe age of 31. Needless to say, they consider themselves happy and contented, even more so than when they were executives in the retail industry, taking home six-digit figures every month.

Like many people, they thought that they would be happy with their lives if they earned five-digit or even six-digit incomes every month. Unlike many people, they were able to achieve the latter. They bought suburban dream houses, luxury cars, and were always equipped with the latest tools and gadgets. Despite all these, they still found themselves like many people in that they were never contented and they found that all the money and the 70-80 hour work weeks were never really enough. Instead of trying to get more to find happiness, they decided to get rid of the things that they had. For Millburn, this meant letting go of his career, his fancy homes and cars, and even his wife of six years. Now, he finds himself happier and more contented than he has ever been, and even he and his ex-wife are now in better terms than they ever have been in the past. Nicodemus went through the same ordeal and quit his job to become a full time blogger. Like Millburn, he is now contented and happy in life, but the road to contentment was never as straightforward as many people think. He had to let go of all devices such as GPS systems and redundant cell phones, along with his position as a corporate executive. He also had to pay off all debts and had to stop himself from spending excessively, including his expenses for his drugs and other addictions.

Both men say that there is nothing inherently wrong about owning things and in fact, they both own iPods and cell phones. According to them, minimalism is not about deprivation but rather about asking yourself, will this decision – buying new things or doing this and that – add real value to my life? Minimalism is not an end-all and be-all but rather a simple tool to clear your life and make it less cluttered so that you do know what is truly important and valuable in life. Less can definitely be more, but once you realize what are truly important – relationships and personal developments – more can also be more.

Chapter 6: How To Use Minimalism To Declutter Your Life And Increase Focus And Productivity

Many people have the idea that minimalists are those who have very little, earn very little, and do very little. On the contrary, minimalists are some of the most successful and productive people who are alive today. As explained in the previous chapters, clutter keeps people from doing what they truly love and from focusing on what are truly important. This is because clutter serves as a distraction. Instead of allowing people to focus on the truly important, clutter only provides stress and puts so many things on our minds simultaneously that we not only lose focus but we also sacrifice our creativity, enthusiasm, and even our positive attitude. All the clutter gives feelings of exhaustion, pressure, and even depression.

The human mind and body is a very remarkable thing. It is said that people only use a small fraction of what they are truly capable of, meaning that we can all be so much more than we are. The only problem is that the world is full of distractions, or so many people say. The reality is that people themselves are the ones who surround themselves with these distractions and clutter that keep them from keeping focus.

Declutter Your Space

One of the most basic things that you can do in order to maintain focus and become more productive is to declutter your space. Have you ever noticed how some offices contain you in small and bland spaces? These spaces contain only the most essential things that you will need to get your job done. In a similar way, you can focus on anything you want to accomplish if you remove the clutter and distractions around you. If you need to study, study in a space where you won't be distracted by the television or the computer or even other books that are unrelated to what you are studying. Movements, sights, and sounds, can all easily distract a person so keep them away and make yourself productive.

Declutter Your Mind

Material things are not the only distractions that keep people from their focus. In fact, even more distracting are the clutter that is in the mind. It is hard to keep focus when the mind is wandering, and it is more often that the mind wanders rather than stays focused on what it needs to. But what are the things that you think about that keep you from being focused? Is it about the date you have after work? The new gadget you have been dying to have? Or the sale at the mall that you have been waiting for all month? These distractions are far from productive, and they also keep you from being more productive as well. Minimalism gives you peace of mind and helps all of these distracting thoughts go away.

Focus

People often lose focus because they think about too many things at once. With minimalism, goals are narrowed down and the mind is freed from distractions. When there is too much to be done and especially when too much is done at once, there is a considerable loss of quality. In most cases, wanting to do too much makes you end up with nothing done at all. At the very least, even if you do accomplish your goals, you may not be a hundred percent satisfied with the outcome. To improve focus, list down the things that you want to do or accomplish. Narrow the list down to the most important and then again to the most urgent. Focus on the urgent and important things first and you will find yourself doing more than if you had tried to do a thousand things at once.

Chapter 7: Minimalism Time Management Strategies To Help You Understand What Is Really Important And What Is Not

Minimalism lets you understand the things that are really important and lets you focus on them so that you realize your goals. While decluttering is one of the most important strategies of a minimalist lifestyle, there are also prioritizing strategies as well as time management strategies that will keep you on the right track.

The Important-Urgent Grid

When it comes to time management strategies, many people are eager to jump at the possibility that they can do more with as little time as possible. While this is indeed ideal, it fails to first address one of the main goals of minimalism, which is to declutter one's life. Time management is not just about doing more, but more so about doing the more important things. In order to do so, one minimalism strategy that you can employ is the important-urgent grid. Do this by drawing a table with two rows and two columns. In the columns heading, write the headers 'urgent' and 'not urgent'. As for the rows, put the headings 'important' and 'not important'. Then, list the things that you want to do or the goals you want to accomplish. Classify your goals into your table, separating the 'important' from the 'not important' and also labeling them as 'urgent' or 'not urgent'. Make sure to set your criteria as to what is considered important and also how urgent your 'urgent' matters are.

Once you have classified your goals into either one of the four spaces, simply cross out the 'not important' row. Writing down your goals helps you to think them through and to realize if you really need to do them or not. By classifying some of your goals as 'not important', you already have a sense that they are mere distractions or clutters in your life. Many of us have these unimportant goals in mind, and the sad part is, people actually focus on these unimportant goals and therefore, they are kept away from the truly important things. Before you try to manage your time, know what is important first.

Prioritizing

After removing the unimportant tasks from your list, focus on whether a goal is urgent or not urgent. Specify your timeframe as well so that you have an idea of how urgent a task should be. Should it be done within the day? A week? This will further help you to understand what the most important of tasks are and what you need to be working on at the soonest possible time. Of course, once you have your goals classified, focus on your important and urgent goals to make sure that you finish them first.

By making the table, you are eliminating or putting off some of your goals in order to make way for and prioritize the more important tasks. People want to do

so much and while this can work out to be productive, proper focus and prioritization can give you more productive and favorable results.

Using A Calendar

Another time management strategy that most minimalists use is the good old calendar method. It is easier to know what is important if you see them written down. Note important dates and schedules on your calendar to make sure that you do not forget them. If the note is a bit more important than the usual, make sure that it stands out by placing markers or using bold and noticeable font. Your calendar or organizer does not have to be too big or elaborate either. In fact, most minimalists prefer pocket-sized organizers or calendars which they can keep at their person at all times. This gives them the chance to bring the calendar anywhere they go, and they can also easily look at the calendar. Make a habit of writing in your calendar if you need any important dates noted, and of course, try to look at your calendar at least once a day.

Making A List

Making a list or putting down notes is an integral part of the strategies noted above that allow minimalists to understand what is really important or not. This only stresses the fact that writing down what you want to do can have a great impact on the way you live. Some people may think that making lists or writing down notes only takes time away from you actually doing what you want to do, but the act of writing actually solidifies the ideas all the more. Most of us start off with thoughts and ideas, and given the amount of distraction that is presented to us every day, these thoughts and ideas can easily get lost or forgotten. The end result is we never work on the goal that we have thought of in the first place, or we start acting on it only to have it half-finished.

Write down your goals and your tasks to strengthen your resolve. By writing them down, you also get the chance to actually think about them and notice if they are indeed important or simply silly whims of the mind. Imagine wanting to do two things: fix your room, and go out and watch a movie. Once written down, you begin to realize that one of those tasks is actually quite shallow. Is it something that really needs to be done, or is it something that you thought of just to pass the time? The mere idea of having to let time pass is very wasteful. Remember that time is something that you cannot take back and once you let it pass, it is gone for good. If you find yourself having time to pass, then that only gives you the opportunity to work on the more important things in life.

Finally, making a list is a way of reminding yourself of the things that need to be done. Distractions are hard to avoid completely and you will find yourself disrupted from the task at hand in one way or another. If you want to finish what you started, write the goals down so that you are reminded of what you have to accomplish. Knowing which goals are important is essential, but acting on them, and seeing them through to the end, is what truly matters.

Chapter 8: Improving Relationships By Learning The Ways Of The Minimalist

Relationships are part of being human, and it seems difficult to think how one can declutter life in terms of these interactions. However, the minimalist way of believing that less is more can also be applied to improving one's relationships. Yes, relationships are normal in life, but not all of them are essential or even good for the person.

Improve your relationships by decluttering them and letting go of the ones that are unhealthy. Those relationships that cause only stress and pain, or even those that only make you feel bad about yourself. Relationships that make you go through such feelings are not worth holding on to. As sad as it may seem, to declutter your life of these relationships means simply to let go of them. Or if possible, realize what relationships are harmful and try to change them into those that are beneficial for you and the others involved.

Letting go of harmful relationships is the easy part. What is harder is cutting down your time from the relationships that you find yourself happy in. Unfortunately, we only have so much time on our hands that we cannot always say yes to everything and everyone. Make sure that you know where your relationships lie on your priority scale. If you have to cut down time from your relationships, know which relationships to cut from and what you are letting go of. Minimalism is not just about saying no, but knowing who to say no to as well as what to say yes to.

While minimalizing your relationships can mean giving up on certain things, it also means that you stand to gain more. Be aware of what you are letting go of and what you are gaining to make it all worth it. Remember that it is about adding value to your life and yourself.

Chapter 9: Allowing Minimalism To Give You Freedom To Travel Or Do The Things Most Important To You

Being more with less and adding value to life by learning to let go are core values of minimalism. It makes one wonder then, how a person is free to do the things he or she wants with such a lifestyle. Minimalists can travel if they want to, they can do the things they enjoy, and they appear to be more free and contented than those who have so much more in life. Many people are curious about the minimalist lifestyle because it appears to bring with it happiness, contentment, and most of all, freedom.

Freedom for a minimalist can come in many forms. For obvious reasons, a minimalist lifestyle allows you to be free from debt and the never-ending cycle of working to buy things but never being satisfied. Of course, minimalism can also free you from needless clutter that fills up the time and efforts of almost everyone in the world.

It is not easy to let go of what minimalists refer to as clutter. Even the home that you are paying a mortgage on or the car that you have on loan is essential for you to live fully and productively. Even the old shirt that you no longer use is hard to get rid of because of some value that it holds. It could be a remembrance or perhaps you simply like it too much to let it go. But again, does holding on to such items add value to life?

Minimalists think differently in that they do not rely on things to add value to their life. They also do not believe that letting go of things means you lose something. On the contrary, the more that minimalists let go of, the more they believe that they gain. They gain freedom from the burden of things, from the stress that they bring, and the pressure to buy even more things that will only bring stress and worry.

A minimalist lifestyle allows you to do simply what you want and to pursue your passions. You do not have to think about paying off your debts and those excessive bills, you feel less pressure of having to buy the latest trends and fashions, and you do not have to waste your time succumbing to the expectations that others have of you. Instead, you realize what is truly valuable, what is most important for you, and you are free to pursue it.

Being a minimalist is not easy. One cannot simply quit a lifelong career and go out travelling or writing blogs and books. Instead, minimalism is a gradual development where one has a clearer picture of what is truly important in life. The less clutter, the clearer life is, and the easier it is to pursue what you find to be important.

Chapter 10: Improving Life By Learning The Ways Of The Minimalist

There may be images and ideas running through your head of what a minimalist is by now. You may imagine them in a small house with the barest of necessities, or that friend who never goes out to the movies with you or eats at the fancy restaurants, or even that person at work who always seems to wear the same blazer, with only a plain shirt underneath that changes color every other day or so. When you think about it however, these minimalists are not too different from you at all. They may make different choices from yours, have different priorities, and definitely follow a different fashion and technological trend, but they are okay nonetheless. In fact, when you get to know them better, you may even find that they are happier, more positive, and a whole lot more contented than any other person you have met.

You do not have to change your whole life abruptly if you want to learn the ways of the minimalist. Change the way you live little by little, and even you can reap the benefits that minimalism can bring.

1. Get rests

    It is easy to say that minimalists declutter their spaces and their lives, but it is harder done. After all, if it were that easy to remove all the distractions and unnecessary things, why wouldn't we all be doing it? The problem again is that there is so much going on that the body and the mind end up getting too stressed. This could probably be the cause of poor judgments or of simply choosing things that will provide momentary comfort when what is actually needed is a more meaningful change. If stress is the problem, then rest is the key. Get rests to rejuvenate the mind and the body. Clear your mind of worries, let your body relax, and simply breathe. A well-rested mind and body even provides enhanced performance, giving you the best results. If you think that you need at least an hour to get meaningful rest, think again as even a 10-minute nap can do wonders for your mind and body.

2. Wake up earlier

   Many of us get things done just in the nick of time. We set our alarm clocks just so we have enough time to get dressed and to go to whatever we need to do during the day, sometimes even pressing the snooze button until we really need to get up lest we be late. Improve your life by waking up earlier. By doing so, you do not have to hurry the moment you wake up. Take your time just walking around, stretching, or even getting yourself that cup of coffee or tea. Even for just fifteen minutes every day, give yourself time to be peaceful and relaxed and you will spend the next 23 hours of the day feeling a whole lot better.

3. Enjoy the outdoors

   Enjoying the outdoors every weekend is a great way to unwind and to remind yourself of the beauty that is around you. On top of this, go outside even during your short breaks during the week or whenever you have the time to. Letting yourself out lets your mind be free from the normal stress and worry that work brings you. The change in environment also fosters a more imaginative and fruitful mind. If the positive mood and atmosphere are not enough, you should also know that the sun and the fresh air does wonders for the mind, the body, and the senses.

4. Turn off the switch

   Gadgets and appliances provide us with ease and convenience. Whenever people have free time on their hands, they turn to these electronic devices that supposedly give them a break from the stress of work and everyday life. Try switching these devices off earlier than you normally would or simply spend less time occupying yourself with the television set, the computer, and the cell phone. Even just 30 minutes of free time away from these gadgets can give your mind the rest that it truly needs. The average person spends at least 30hours per week watching the television, and even more hours glued to computer screens and mobile devices. Imagine what you could do if you decided to turn off the switch and focus on more important things.

5. Take longer to eat, or to shower

   Slowing down, taking deep breaths, and simply relaxing, are great ways to rid yourself of distractions and clutters that make your life a mess. Take your time when you eat, when you shower, or whenever you give time for yourself to let your mind be clear of distractions. Do not worry that giving yourself more time will reduce the output you are able to produce as the more rested your mind and body is, the better their outcome can be. Be more efficient and let your mind relax.

Conclusion

Life can be full of distractions but we can be free of them if we choose. Learn to say no and to free yourself, to slow down and let yourself relax, and to be mindful of and happy about the more important things in life.

Thank you again for purchasing this book *minimalist* I believe it will help make you happier and more productive!

I am extremely excited to pass this information along to you, and I am so happy that you now have read and can hopefully implement these strategies going forward.

I hope this book was able to help you understand that there is more to life than all the luxuries and conveniences that money can buy, and how to free your mind and yourself from all the clutter that keeps you from realizing the person that you can be.

The next step is to get started using this information and to hopefully live a happier, more content, and more productive life!

Please don't be someone who just reads this information and doesn't apply it, the strategies in this book will only benefit you if you use them!

If you know of anyone else that could benefit from the information presented here please inform them of this book.

Finally, if you enjoyed this book and feel it has added value to your life in any way, please take the time to share your thoughts and post a review on Amazon. It'd be greatly appreciated!

Thank you and good luck!

Preview Of:

Ultimate Manifestation Guide!

<u>Manifestation</u>

The Science Of Manifestation Through Neuroplasticity, Brain Training, NLP Techniques, Creative Visualization, Mindfulness Meditation, And More!

Introduction

I want to thank you and congratulate you for purchasing the book, *"Manifestation: Ultimate Manifestation Guide! The Science Of Manifestation Through Neuroplasticity, Brain Training, NLP Techniques, Creative Visualization, Mindfulness Meditation, And More!"*

This book contains proven steps and strategies on how to use manifestation techniques to attract the things that you want in life. This book will help you understand the universal law of attraction and help you use it to transform your dreams into reality.

If you feel that your life is getting nowhere and you feel that you cannot control the outcome of your life, this book is for you. This book will help you understand the power of your mind to change your life for the better. This book will also help you realize that you are the master of your life and you have the creative power to map out your destiny.

Thanks again for purchasing this book, I hope you enjoy it!

Chapter 1: Proof That Manifestation Is Real

The law of attraction is quite popular nowadays. Many celebrities believe it and many claim that they have used it to achieve success and personal transformation. But is it really real?

Well, the law of attraction is a universal law that states that the more you think about something, the more it manifests in your life. So, if you think about success often, if you believe that you are destined for success, you will eventually achieve success. If you think about failure, on the other hand, you will attract people and circumstances that will orchestrate to deliver what you expect – failure.

Have you noticed that whenever you think about a person that you have not thought about for years, he suddenly shows up days later? Have you noticed that if you express interest on, say, traveling to Paris, you will begin to see airline ads and deals that would help you realize your Paris dream vacation? That's huge proof that the law of manifestation is real.

To further illustrate this point, let's take a look at the success stories of celebrities who have deliberately used the law of attraction to bring success into their lives. In the 1980s, Jim Carrey was a struggling actor. He was constantly depressed and he has a hard time trying to make ends meet. He has read about the law of attraction and he decided to give it a try. He wrote himself a check worth ten million dollars and dated the check 1995. He kept the check in his wallet for years. He had nearly forgotten about it. In 1994, Jim Carrey got his breakout roles as Ace Ventura: The Pet Detective and as The Mask. Because of the success of these two films, his market value have significantly increased and he received a ten million dollar check in 1994 for his acting service in the film "Dumb and Dumber".

In 1985, Oprah Winfrey read the book called "The Color Purple". She never stopped thinking about the book and she was literally addicted to it. Years later, her agent called and said that she got an audition for the movie adaptation of "The Color Purple". She wanted the part so bad that she regularly prayed for it. She visualized herself going to the set and shooting the film. She waited for the callback for months and finally, she got the part. Oprah said that the fact that she wanted the part so bad and she believed that she can achieve it and that she is worthy of it is the starting point of her successful career.

The power of thought to influence manifestation was also proven by the water experiment conducted by Dr. Emoto Masaru. Dr. Masaru and his team studies the molecular structure of normal water when frozen. They then asked a monk to bless a glass of water with gratitude and love. They froze the water and they were surprised to see that the molecular structure of the water that was blessed by the monk is different from the unblessed water. The water that was exposed to feelings of love, gratitude, and peace have a beautiful flower-like molecular structure. They then exposed another glass of water to music that is full of angst and hatred. They were also shock to find out that the water exposed to anger have a distorted and ugly molecular form.

The result of this experiment is proof that our thoughts and emotions influence our outer or physical reality. Remember that our body and the world are mainly made of water. Notice that if you wake up in the morning feeling cranky, you will attract negative circumstances because you have emitted negative vibes. If you wake up thinking that it is going to be a bad day, well, it is definitely going to be a bad day. The universe will deliver whatever you expect.

The law of attraction is real and it has helped many people achieve the life that they have always dreamed of. Now is the time for you to use it to your advantage and achieve everything that you have hoped for.

Thanks for Previewing My Exciting Book Entitled:

"Manifestation: Ultimate Manifestation Guide! The Science Of Manifestation Through Neuroplasticity, Brain Training, NLP Techniques, Creative Visualization, Mindfulness Meditation, And More!"

To purchase this book, simply go to the Amazon Kindle store and simply search:

"MANIFESTATION"

Then just scroll down until you see my book. You will know it is mine because you will see my name "Ryan Cooper" underneath the title.

Alternatively, you can visit my author page on Amazon to see this book and other work I have done. Thanks so much, and please don't forget your free bonuses

DON'T LEAVE YET! - CHECK OUT YOUR FREE BONUSES BELOW!

Free Bonus Offer: Get Free Access To The www.LuxyLifeNaturals.com VIP Newsletter!

Once you enter your email address you will immediately get free access to this awesome newsletter!

But wait, right now if you join now for free you will also get free access to the "Anti-Aging Made Easy" free EBook!

To claim both your FREE VIP NEWSLETTER MEMBERSHIP and your FREE BONUS Ebook on ANTI-AGING MADE EASY!

Just Go To:

www.LuxyLifeNaturals.com

www.ingramcontent.com/pod-product-compliance
Lightning Source LLC
Chambersburg PA
CBHW070939290526
45795CB00003B/1072